For a better life
Divine Grace

A Book on Self-Empowerment

Compiled by
M. M. Walia

NEW DAWN PRESS, INC.
USA • UK • INDIA

NEW DAWN PRESS GROUP

Published by New Dawn Press Group
New Dawn Press, Inc., 244 South Randall Rd # 90, Elgin, IL 60123
e-mail: sales@newdawnpress.com

New Dawn Press, 2 Tintern Close, Slough, Berkshire, SL1-2TB, UK
e-mail: salesuk@newdawnpress.org

New Dawn Press (An Imprint of Sterling Publishers (P) Ltd)
A-59, Okhla Industrial Area, Phase-II, New Delhi-110020, India
e-mail: info@sterlingpublishers.com
www.sterlingpublishers.com

For a better life – Divine Grace

© 2006, Sterling Publishers (P) Ltd
ISBN 1 84557 575 X

All rights are reserved. No part of this publication may be
reproduced, stored in a retrieval system or transmitted, in any
form or by any means, mechanical, photocopying, recording or
otherwise, without prior written permission of the publisher.

PRINTED IN INDIA

Amazing Grace

Amazing grace! How sweet the sound
That saved a wretch like me!
I once was lost, but now am found,
Was blind, but now I see.
'Twas grace that taught my heart to fear,
And grace my fears relieved;
How precious did that grace appear
The hour I first believed!
Through many dangers, toils and snares,
I have already come;
'Tis grace that brought me safe thus far,
And grace will lead me home.

And when we've been there ten thousand years,
Bright shining as the sun,
We'll have no less days to sing God's praise
Than when we'd first begun.

– John Newton

He Answers My Prayers

I asked God for strength, that I might achieve.
I was made weak, that I might learn to obey...
I asked for health, that I might do great things.
I was given infirmity, that I might do better...
I asked for riches, that I might be happy.
I was given poverty, that I might be wise...
I asked for power, that I might be praised by men.

I was given weakness, that I might feel the need of God...

I asked for all things, that I might enjoy life.

I was given life, that I might enjoy all things...

I got nothing I asked for — but everything I had hoped for.

Almost despite myself, my unspoken prayers were answered.

I am, among men, most richly blessed!

— *Ray Camapanella*

Without the benefit
of Divine Grace,
man can achieve really
nothing.

The first step to appreciate the infinite power of Divine Grace is to have faith in divine power or even the belief in the existence of God.

The genesis of Divine Grace lies, first of all, in accepting the limitless powers of this Divine entity.

> Success in life
> is a multiple of
> two basic factors –
> Self-effort and Divine
> Grace.
> – M. M. Walia

Sri Aurobindo and The Mother on Divine Grace

What is Grace?

The dictionary meaning of the word 'Grace' is: 'unmerited favour of God'; 'Divine regeneration; and inspiring and strengthening influence'. In the *Gita*, it is referred to as *'prasada'*. The word *prasada* means favour, kindness, propitiousness, graciousness of disposition. The other word conveying the same sense is *'anugraha'*.

The term Grace covers a vast panorama of meanings. *'Kripa'* is the loving and compassionate intervention of God in human affairs. *'Anugraha'* is an unconditional initiative on the part of the Divine, who takes charge and transforms that part common to man and God (anu). *Prasada* is the state of supreme peace fulfilment in vedantic tradition, and *Param Shanti*, the peace that passeth all understanding when we attain union with Him.

Grace is something freely given, not taken as a right. There is no quid pro quo or measure in it. The Lord gives out of His sweet will and pleasure. You cannot demand it as rightful dues. This implies that Grace transcends the law. Explaining Divine Grace Sri Sankara says in the Gita Bhashya — Grace is the redemptive power of the Lord.

If we remember this definition, the various conundrums about Grace will stand resolved. The Lord is ever bountiful to shower his blessings on the votary.

The Grace of the Divine involves a two-fold movement, one from the seeker towards God, and the other from God towards the seeker. It is something called the ascent of man and the descent of God.

Grace and Devotion

The concept of Grace is integrally linked with devotion. Through devotion, the devotee clings wholeheartedly to a merciful and responsive God and offers his all to his beloved Divinity. His self-surrendering attitude opens his heart to the reception of the fullness of Divine

Grace. According to a staunch theist, even this attitude of self-surrender is a precious gift of God.

Grace is perfect when, instead of looking for Grace from Him, we Gracefully surrender ourselves, for Him to use us as He wills.

Grace stands for Divine Mercy and karma for Divine Justice. It is sometimes believed that the theories of Karma and Divine Grace are opposed to each other. Followers of the path of devotion traditionally hold Grace supreme. Both theories have been subjected to the criticism of being fatalistic and deterministic, leaving no room for self-effort or free-will. Careful examination will reveal that the two theories are complementary, and that both theories admit the necessity of self-effort for spiritual progress.

Grace and Logic

Divine Grace is not something like a Divine reason, acting on logical, intelligent lines, as understood by the human mind. Many a time one can find no rhyme or reason for its action, cause or motive. Therefore, some would like to interpret Divine as *karuna* or *kripa* of the Lord, a sort of Universal Divine Compassion.

But the action of Grace need not always be kindly. A calamity or catastrophe that happens to an aspirant is proved by subsequent events to be a gift of Grace from the Divine. Therefore, Divine Grace cannot be equated with Divine Compassion. As Sri Aurobindo says, "One cannot demand Grace as a right and privilege — for then it would not be Grace."

So, can we say that Divine Grace is nothing but Divine Caprice? Not at all, it is never capricious. It has its own law of action, far superior to the law of Cause and Effect, on Karma, which is even beyond the ken of the Cosmic Law. Only this law is unintelligible to the human mind. So, the action of Grace is hailed as miraculous, and mysterious.

A perfect openness and absolute sincerity is required on the part of the *receiver*. The Guru or the Divine is ready to pour down Grace; but the *receiver* should lay his being open to the play of Grace. Grace is like sunlight; if one chooses, one can close the windows and doors and be content to remain in darkness. If the *Sadhaka* is closed and petty, there is no use blaming Grace for not acting. Therefore, Sri Aurobindo warns: "Few are those from whom Grace withdraws, but many are those who withdraw from Grace."

Grace and Self Effort

God can also be compared to the wind; when we mend a hole in the sail, our boat is propelled by the wind. Make the effort and you will realise the power of Grace.

If everything is destined, where does God's Grace come in? The answer is that one must sit with a fishing rod if one wants to catch fish. In spiritual progress, God makes us work a bit, and then He does the rest. We must take the first step, then He comes ten steps.

Conditions for Receiving Grace

The conditions for Grace are best summarised in the concluding verses of the eighteenth chapter of the *Gita*: The Lord said: "Ever performing all work always, taking refuge in Me, he (the devotee) attains through My Grace the eternal and immutable state. Resigning mentally all actions to Me, regarding me as the supreme goal, and resorting to Yoga through the intellect, ever fix your mind on Me. Fixing your mind on Me, you will overcome all difficulties through My Grace. But if from self-conceit, you do not listen to Me, you will perish. The Lord dwells in the heart of all beings, O Arjuna, and by His *maya* causes them to revolve as though mounted on a machine. Take refuge in Him alone with all your heart, O Bharata. By His Grace you will gain supreme peace and eternal abode."

The second condition is resorting to what is called *Buddhi*-Yoga or work done through wisdom. This wisdom of Yoga is one of the topics discussed in the second part of the second chapter, when the Lord introduces the subject of Karma Yoga.

This, in short, is to perform actions, giving up attachment, and without concern as to success or failure. Work done through wisdom, giving up the fruits of action, is superior to that prompted by desire. Hence, the lord repeatedly urges Arjuna to take refuge in this wisdom.

The third condition is to fix the mind on the lord: *Matchittah*. This amounts to concentration, described in detail in the sixth chapter. The path of concentration has certain preliminaries, like the selection of a clean secluded spot, spreading the prescribed seat and sitting on it in a firm, erect posture. The internal and the essential aspect of this practice, however, consists in controlling the mind and fixing it on the Lord.

Result of Grace

The fortunate recipient of Divine Grace attains eternal abode and supreme peace. This is also called the Brahmi state obtained by a man of steady wisdom, and a devotee who has transcended the three *gunas*. Being established in this state, a devotee becomes liberated in his lifetime, and after death attains Brahma Nirvana. If a devotee does not aspire for this state of the highest spiritual illumination, he, by the Lord's Grace, is freed from all sins and difficulties. His delusion is destroyed, he strengthens his memory, and is able to perceive his duty clearly. Thus, Grace is conducive to the spiritual as well as to the material welfare of a devotee.

Grace in Christian Theology

To the Catholic, Grace is ethical in aim and charged with a mysteriously sanctifying power. To the evangelical Prostestant, Grace is the free active love of God for sinners, which was so personally present in Christ as to elicit faith by its intrinsically persuasive content. However, in a heartfelt confession expressing man's utter indebtedness to God, Saint Paul says: "By the Grace of God, I am what I am."

Religion begins when we encounter a Power within, which subdues us purely by its sweet and overpowering presence — a presence which does not destroy freedom but raises it to its highest point. It is not so much a question, then, of shutting out all other influences, but opening and expanding our nature so as to receive the loftiest experience: only through Grace do we become personalities in the highest and fullest sense. Grace changes our lifestyle; the self is no more the centre, and so that taint of egoism and self-righteousness cannot adhere to our thoughts and action.

Jesus upheld the doctrine of divine Grace when he declared: "Many are called, but few are chosen." Through self-effort we ourselves must choose to be chosen by God.

Grace is that Power which the seeker feels as unconditional, bountiful, and benevolent, coming in various ways and helping him at every step. Initially, he considers the help he receives, whether solicited, in the course of his spiritual practices, to be coming from an unaccountable source and being conferred on him regardless of his merit. This alone he calls Divine Grace. As he progresses along the path, however, his insight deepens. He comes to feel that whatever results come to him according to the law of causation, are due to that Divine Power. The existence of cosmic law, which enables him to struggle spiritually in a methodical way, he now perceives as Divine Grace too. Later when he becomes spiritually mature, that is, when he sees God face to face, he recognises that everything — his own initiative, past or present, the inspiration imbibed from spiritual teachers, all aspects of spiritual endeavour, and his final realisation — is possible only because of this gracious Divine Power.

Divine Grace Through Surrender

The Divine gives itself to those who give themselves without reserve. For them it is the calm, the light, the power, the bliss, the freedom, the wideness, the heights of knowledge, the seas of *Ananda*.

Always keep in touch with the Divine Force. The best thing for you is to allow it to do its own work; wherever necessary, it will take hold of the inferior energies and purify them; at other times it will empty you of them and fill you with itself. But if you let your mind take the lead and discuss and decide what is to be done, you will lose touch with the Divine Force and the lower energies will begin to act for themselves and all will go into confusion.

All can be done by the Divine — the heart and nature purified, the inner consciousness awakened, the veils removed — if one gives oneself to the

Divine with trust and confidence, and even if one cannot do so fully at once, yet the more one does so, the more the inner help and guidance will come and the experience of the Divine grows within. If the questioning mind becomes less active and if humility and the will to surrender grows, this ought to be perfectly possible. No other strength and *tapasya* are then needed, but this alone.

Some Famous Mystics on Divine Grace.

"It is the Power,
the Happiness,
the Light,
the Knowledge,
the Beatitude,
the Love and Peace which
come to us from Divine Grace."

– *The Mother*

All you have been, and seen, and done, and thought,
Not you, but I have seen and been and wrought...
Pilgrim, pilgrimage, and road,
Was but myself at my own door...
Come, you lost atoms, to your centre draw...
Rays that have wandered into darkness wide,
Return, and back into your Sun subside.

— *Mantiqu't-Tair*

Very right is thy faith and pride in His Grace,
And true it is that it works
Like rain shower on a tilled field.
But to what avail all shower,
If ye have not sown the field?

— Sheikh Sa'di

If I were pure, never shall I taste the sweets
of the forgiveness of sins.
If I were holy, I could never behold the tears.
O! Love, Mercy! O divine humility!
O Forgiveness! O! Pity and Compassion!
If I were pure, I should never have known
Thee...

Would Thou love one who never died for Thee;
or even die for one who had not died for Thee?
And if God dieth not for man
and giveth not Himself
Eternally for man, man could not exist;
For Man is love, as God is love,
Every kindness to another is a little death.
In the Divine Image none can exist but by brotherhood.

— *Sufi Sarmad*

His grace may fall on us at any time.
There is no definite rule regulating it.
Some do not get it even after performing great austerities and night long vigils,
Whilst it is forced on those who lie asleep.

— Baba Farid

Ah! How merciful is He that He ordered my head to be severed from my body!
From a serious headache I was suffering,
He cut the matter short!
The incident of Mansur was forgotten through passage of time,
By ordering my crucifixion,

once more He renewed the Tale of Great Love!

— *Sufi Mansur*

"If birth, actions, age (youth), physical beauty, knowledge, etc., do not cause arrogance in anyone, (know that) that is the sign of my Grace."

— *Lord Vishnu "Sri Bhagvatam"*

"Even to turn towards God, or striving towards liberation, man needs His Grace".

— *Vedanta Philosophy*

Sri Ramakrishna On Divine Grace

The wind of God's Grace is incessantly blowing. Lazy sailors on the sea of life do not take advantage of it. But the active and the strong always keep the sails of their minds unfurled to catch the favourable wind, and thus reach their destination very soon.

You may try thousands of times, but nothing can be achieved without God's Grace. One cannot see God without His Grace. Is it an easy thing to receive the

Grace of God? One must altogether renounce egotism; one cannot see God as long as one feels superior.

God does not really appear in the heart of a man who feels himself to be his own master. But God can be seen the moment His Grace descends. He is the Sun of knowledge. One single ray of His has illuminated the world with the light of knowledge. That is how we are able to see one another and acquire varied knowledge. One can see God only if He turns His light towards His own face.

The police sergeant goes on his rounds in the dark of the night with a lantern in his hand. No one sees his face; but, with the help of that light, the sergeant sees everybody's face, and others, too, can see one another. If you want to see the sergeant, however, you must pray to him: "Sir, please turn the light on your own face. Let me see you." In the same way, one must pray to God: "O Lord, be gracious and turn the light of knowledge on Thyself that I may see Thy face."

The doubts of the mind will not disappear without His Grace. Doubts will not disappear without self-realisation.

But one need not fear anything if one has received the Grace of God. It is easy for a child to stumble if *he* holds his father's hand: but there can be no such fear if the father holds the child's hand. A man does not have to suffer any more if God, in His Grace, removes man's doubts and reveals Himself to him. But this Grace descends upon man only after he has prayed to God with intense yearning in his heart and practised spiritual discipline. A mother feels compassion for her child when she sees him running about breathlessly.

"But why should God make us run about?" It is His will that we should run about a little. God has created the world like a play. This is called *Mahamaya*- the Great Illusion.

Four Types of Surrender

The first type is that of a fish taken out of water. This is not a safe one. Like a fish, if taken out of water, will die, so also an aspirant here, who loses the company or communion or association of a saint will fall down immediately from his path.

The higher and the better type of surrender than this is that of a monkey. If a baby monkey stops its effort of clinging to its mother, it will immediately fall down, losing its grip. Hence, like a baby monkey, we have to exert our own personal efforts in holding or clinging onto our divine mother.

The third is that of the cat type. Here the efforts to guard the baby are made by the mother singularly. The baby is carefree. It may not even fully cooperate with its mother. The mother cat takes the baby to various places and at last at a proper time, the baby opens its eyes. However, not knowing exactly the motivation or ideas of its mother, the baby may try to escape from its mother's grip; and when the mother tightens its grip, the baby may suffer from the hard hold of its mother.

The above types of surrender are not complete. The fourth and final type is the hen type. In the hen type of surrender, the mother hen puts in all efforts to look after her kids. She feeds them, guards them, guides them to live together as fully co-operative members of a single family, and teaches them so that they can behave nicely as members of a unified family. By her training, efforts and guidance she imparts the knowledge of team spirit, cooperation, and friendliness into them, so that each individual of her family becomes the complete unite of *Suhridbhava*. All these things are directed not by force but by divine love without any expectation and without any trace of rejection or avoidance. Here the baby is completely safeguarded all the time. What it has to do is to remain in the presence of its mother and also with its companions. The *Sambabdha* Yoga is the main aspect here. All the divine qualities are naturally imparted to the child by the mother under full protection, control, care and supervision.

The fourth type of surrender is the best, supreme, simple and easy. It leads to total vision. The multi-dimensional character of the dynamic divine life of a *Sadhaka* is easily built up here, because here is the best combination of *Svadharma* and *Suhridbhava* mutually with one another.

— *Brahm Swarup P. P. Kakaji*

Divine Grace and Karma Philosophy

Grace stands for Divine Mercy and *karma* for Divine Justice. It is sometimes believed that the theories of karma and Divine Grace are opposed to each other. Followers of the path of devotion, traditionally hold Grace supreme. *Avatars* are the tangible manifestation of that Grace. Buddhists, Jains and Jnanis stress the inexorable law of karma. Both theories have been subjected to the criticism of being fatalistic and deterministic, leaving no room for self-effort or free-will. Careful examination will reveal that the two theories are complementary, and that both theories admit the necessity of self-effort for spiritual progress.

The most satisfactory working solution will have to fall somewhere between the extremes of the Karma theory and Grace. Holy Mother Sarada Devi gives a beautiful illustration. If a man was destined to lose his leg because of his past Karma, he will escape with only a scratch by calling on the Lord. Or, as Sri Ramakrishna said, there is free-will in man, but it has a limit. A cow is tied to a post with a rope twenty yards long. The cow is free within twenty yards, but not beyond that. Similarly, a man is not absolutely free; he is controlled either by his Karma or by God. By self-effort he can greatly change the course of his life or accelerate his spiritual progress, as can be done in a film. Karma, in the form of spiritual practices and meaningful experiences, is an aspect of gace. And grace may be seen as a manifestation of previous Karma. Sri Ramakrishna says, if you take ten steps towards Mother, Mother takes a hundred steps towards you. So some effort has to be made to make the mother know that we are no more satisfied with our dolls, but are anxious to have Her alone. And then, She in Her grace comes to us.

— *Swami Swahananda*

"We sleep in peace in the arms of God when we yield ourselves up to His providence, in a delightful consciousness of His tender mercies; no more restless uncertainties, no more anxious desires, no more impatience at the place we are in; for it is God who has put us there, and who holds us in his arms. Can we be unsafe where He has placed us?"

– Fenelon

The Grace of the Guru

There is no knowledge without the Guru, no discipline without the Guru. No love will arise in the heart without the Guru. Without the Guru your intellect is not illumined, nor is your delusion removed.

Without the Guru you cannot attain the highest state – God realisation.

Therefore, it is essential to attain the Grace of the Guru.

– *The Poet Surdas*

Forgive me when I whine

And then I stopped to buy some sweets.
The lad who sold them had such charm.
I talked with him – he said to me:
'It's nice to talk to folks like you,
You see,' he said, 'I'm blind.'
Oh, God, forgive me when I whine;
I have two eyes – the world is mine!
Then, walking down the street,
I saw a child with eyes of blue.
He stood and watched the others play;
It seemed he knew not what to do.

I stopped a moment, when I said:
'Why don't you join the others, dear?'
He looked ahead without a word,
And then I knew he could not hear.
Oh, God, forgive me when I whine;
I have two ears – the world is mine!
With feet to take me where I want to go,
With eyes to see the sunset's glow,
With ears to hear what I would know,
Oh, God forgive me when I whine;
I'm blessed, indeed! The world is mine!

— *Anonymous*

The Meaning of Guru

❖ The word Guru consists of two syllabus "Gu" meaning darkness and "ru" meaning light. It is Guru who destroys the darkness of ignorance and misunderstanding and puts his disciples in contact with the divine light of wisdom and knowledge.

❖ It is important to understand that the Guru is not merely a human being in this physical form. He is the representation of God's power of Grace. The "Shive Sutra Vimarshini" says the "Guru is the Grace-bestowing power of God".

❖ Such a Guru has the power to bestow Grace, and has the ability to transmit God's energy to others. By awakening the inner power, the Guru removes ignorance and dissolves false pride and ego which prevents one from realising the existence of God within oneself.

❖ In order to attain the full Grace of the Guru, we have to become His devotees and surrender ourselves to the Guru without reservation, so that He can work on us to dissolve our ego and pride, because our spiritual life and progress depends completely on the Guru.

The Greatness of the Guru

❖ The Guru Gita describes the importance of devotion to the Guru, his/her qualities and attributes, and the status of the Guru. The holy book emphasises that realisation of God is possible only through a Guru because He is Parabrahma, one who is worthy of being worshipped and being meditated upon.

❖ Our culture and scriptures have placed great emphasis on the status of the Guru. The Guru is ranked equal to the trinity God-Heads — Lord Brahma, the creator of the Universe; Lord Vishnu, the provider, maintainer and protector of the Universe; and Lord Maheshwara, the destroyer of ignorance and negativity.

❖ The Guru, through his/her deep meditation, penance, and powers generates and creates new thoughts, ideas, ideals and values. Through his/her pious lifestyle, Grace and compassion he/she fosters, inspires, and promotes peace, tranquillity and harmony to enrich the culture.

- ❖ The Guru destroys the ignorance in our life and restores morals and tradition in our society, and hence taking on the role of Lord Maheshwara, to crush the *Tamas* nature of ignorance.

Serving the Guru

❖ "It is by the Grace of the Guru and only through service to the Guru that Brahma, Vishnu and Shiva become capable of creation, sustenance and destruction." Guru Seva, selfless service to the Guru, is one of the most important means of *sadhana* (spiritual practice) to gain the Guru's Grace. It is only through the Guru's Grace and service that devotion, bhakti, and knowledge arise.

— *Brahmajyoti*

Gems of Wisdom from Sri Sathya Sai Baba

❖ The most desirable form of wealth is the Grace of God. He will guard you even as lids guard the eyes. Do not doubt this faith in providence which is the very breath of life.

❖ Hear good things, see good, do good, think good; then you get the Grace of God, as all the evil tendencies will be uprooted.

❖ God's Grace is the shower of rain, is the sunlight. You have to do some *sadhana* to acquire it; the *sadhana* of keeping a pot upright to receive the rain, the *sadhana* of opening the door of your heart so that the sun may illumine it.

❖ Your progress is reflected back as Grace. Your decline is reflected as its absence. The mirror just reflects. It has no partiality or prejudice.

❖ If complete faith is placed in the Lord at all times, why should He deny you

His Grace? Why should He desist from helping you? Men do not rely fully and unswervingly on the Lord.

❖ Cultivate faith and surrender; then, Grace will flow through you into every act of yours, for, they are no longer your acts, they are His, and you have no concern about the consequence thereof. All acts, words and thoughts will thereafter be pure, saturated with love and conducive to peace. Cleanse your hearts so that the Lord may be reflected therein, in all

His Splendour, in all His myriad forms.

❖ The Grace of the Lord will overwhelm all obstacles. It is Grace that gives value to life.

❖ *Anushithanam* brings about *Anugraham*. Act and earn Grace.

❖ Everyone has the right to earn the Grace of God. This is your birthright.

Gems of Wisdom from Thomas A Kempis

Those who attribute to God all the good they have received, do not seek glory from another, but they want that glory which comes from God alone; and above all, they desire that God be praised in them and in all the Saints, and they always aim at this.

Be grateful then for every little thing, and you will be worthy to receive greater things. Regard the least gift as great, and the most common as a special gift. If you consider the dignity of the giver, no gift will seem little which is given by the most high God. And even when he inflicts punishment and stripes, it should be acceptable to us; for whatever he permits he always does it for our salvation.

He who desires to retain in himself the Grace of God, let him be thankful for the Grace given and resigned for that which is withdrawn. Let him pray to receive it; let him be cautious and humble so as not to lose it again.

Your profit in the spiritual life does not come only when you have the Grace of consolation, but when, with humility and abnegation, you patiently bear having it taken away from you; so that then you do not grow tepid in your love of prayer, nor permit to omit any of your accustomed good works.

God often gives, in one short moment, what he has for a long time denied.

Therefore, humble and mortify yourself that you may receive the Grace of devotion.

The Mother on Faith and Grace

The Extent of Grace

No matter how great your faith and trust in Divine Grace, no matter how great your capacity to see it at work in all circumstances, at every moment, at every point of life, you will never succeed in understanding the marvellous immensity of Its Action, and the precision, the exactitude with which this Action is accomplished; you will never be able to grasp to what extent Grace does everything, is behind everything, organises everything, conducts everything, so that the march forward to the divine realisation may be as swift, as complete, as total and harmonious as possible, considering the circumstances of the world.

As soon as you are in with it, there is not a second in time, not a point in space, which does not show you *dazzlingly* this perpetual work of Grace, this constant intervention of Grace.

And once you have seen this, you feel you are never equal to it, for you should never forget it, never have any fears, any anguish, any regrets, any recoils... or even suffering. If one were in union with this Grace, if one saw It everywhere, one would begin living a life of exultation, of all-power, of infinite happiness.

The Need for Grace

The most important point is to have a certain inner humility which makes you aware of your helplessness without Grace, that truly, without it you are incomplete and powerless. This, to begin with, is the first thing.

And then, if you become aware that it is only Grace which can do what you cannot do, Grace alone can pull you out of the situation in which you find yourself, can give you the solution and the strength to come out of it. Then, quite naturally, an intense aspiration awakens in you, a consciousness which is translated into an opening. If you call, and if you hope to get an answer, you will quite naturally open yourself to Grace.

And Grace will answer you, It will pull you out of trouble, Grace will give you the solution to your problem. But once you are free from trouble and have come out of your difficulty, do not forget that it is Grace which pulled you out. And do not think it is yourself.

The moment you think that you are the one who has accomplished things, you lock the door, and you cannot receive anything any more. You need, once again, some acute anguish, some terrible difficulty for this kind of inner stupidity to give way, and for you to realise once more that you can do nothing on your own. Because it is only when you grow aware that you are powerless that you begin to be just a little open and plastic. But so long as you think that what you do depends on your own skill and your own capacity, truly, not only do you close one door, but, you know, you close lot of doors one upon another, and bolt them. You shut yourself up in a fortress and nothing can enter there.

Grace and the Sinner

Grace helps the sinner to give up his sin. It does not push away the sinner, saying, "I won't do anything for you." It is there always, even when he is sinning, to help him to come out; not to continue in his sin.

God never rejects us. His Grace is there even with the worst of criminals, to help them change.

Identify With Grace

It is Divine Grace which makes you progress, and with Divine Grace you feel Divine Joy. But instead of identifying yourself with Grace which makes you progress, you identify yourself with the ugly thing you want to get rid of; and so, naturally, you feel like it and suffer.

If you identify yourself with the Divine Force which comes to liberate you, you feel the joy of Divine Grace — and you experience the deep delight of the progress you have made.

And this is a sign for you, a sure indication of what you identify yourself with. If you are identified with the forces from below, you suffer, if you are identified with the forces from above, you are happy.

Making the Connection

God is always there. But you have to reach forward to receive His help. That is why the *Bible* says, "Ask and you shall receive." He will not come by force to help you. You must ask for His mercy, or blessings. His Grace is everywhere. It's not that He selects people and says, "I will bless this one and not that one." He and His creation, which you call nature, are always neutral.

But to become ready to receive His help you need His Grace. Sri Ramakrishna once gave a beautiful example:

There were a few fishermen preparing to go to sea early one morning. Within half an hour they were ready and all the boats were sailing out — except one.

The sailor of that boat complained: What is this? My boat is not moving. All the others are sailing fine. The wind seems to be partial. It gives its force to those boats but not to mine.

As he was blaming the wind, a person standing on the shore called to him: "Say, what is this? They have all unfurled their sails and caught the wind. But you haven't opened yours."

"Oh, I see. I'll do that." He opened his sail and immediately the boat went forward, but then stopped. He stood up and shouted, "See, I told you. It is partial. I think it has some kind of grievance against me. You told me to open my sail. I did that and it moved a little, but now I am stuck again. What can I do now?"

"Friend, you are quick to blame others. You don't want to see your mistake. Did you pull up your anchor?"

"Ahh. I see. I am terribly sorry." And the minute he pulled up the anchor, he sailed on.

God is like that. He wants to bless you, but He can't force Himself in. He waits for you to be ready, for you to ask, for you to open your mind. That is why the scriptures say that even a camel can pass through the eye of a needle before God can come into the millionaire's mind.

"Lord, by myself I have no capacity to ask anything of You. Without Your blessings and Your Grace, I cannot even pray."

—Swami Satchinanda

Divine Grace and the Holy Gita

To a true believer, every word of the *Gita* is divine and the book is Divine Grace by itself. The most appropriate shloka is the last shloka, quoted below: "Where Krishna is the Lord of Yoga, wherever Partha is the archer, there is prosperity, victory, happiness, and sound policy; this is my conviction."

– *Sanjay (78/XVIII)*

Here, it is important to note that the presence of Yogeshwarah Krishna is an inescapable prerequisite for any successful endeavour, but without the warrior prince Arjuna, who is armed and ready to fight, nothing is likely to be achieved. So just by mere spiritually and without physical effort, no worthwhile achievement is possible.

The paramount significance of the 'firm/steady/sound policy' emphasised in this all-important concluding stanza of the *Gita*, is indeed noteworthy. Its relevance exists at the individual as well as the state level.

"Strength, if it is spiritual, is a power for spiritual realisation; a greater power is sincerity; the greatest power of all is Grace."

I have said times without number that if a man is sincere, he will overcome difficulties. I have repeatedly spoken of Divine Grace. I have referred any number of times to the line from the *Gita*:

"I will deliver thee from all sin and evil; do not grieve."

— *Sri Aurobindo*

Islam and Divine Grace

Islam spells out specific acts by man to avail His Grace. These are:

The Holy Kalima

There is no God save one God, and Mohammad is His Apostle. The first step to avail His Grace requires total faith in this basic tenet of Islam.

Namaz

When a person stands before the Almighty with his arms folded, five times a day, and celebrates His praises and kneels down before

Him, touches the ground with his forehead and makes earnest supplications to Him, he becomes worthy of His Grace.

Zakat

It requires spending a certain portion of one's wealth for the poor and the needy.

Roza

Fasting is meant to promote piety and righteousness in man. It teaches him self-control, and discipline over his carnal needs.

Haj

Those who can afford to make the Pilgrimage for Haj are God's guests and their petitions will be granted.

The five fundamentals of the teaching of Islam outlined above are known as the five Pillars of the Faith. Sincere observance of these tenets is the surest way to receive Divine Grace.

Great stress has also been laid on singing constant praises of God, on supplication through prayer and repentance, by seeking His forgiveness and mercy.

Quotes from the Bible

- For by Grace you have been saved through faith; and this is not your own doing, it is the gift of God.

    – Ephesians 2:8

- God is our refuge and strength, a very present help in trouble.

    – Psalm 46:1

- With men this is impossible, but with God all things are possible.
  – *Matthew 29:26*
- Commit your way to the Lord and he will crown your efforts with success.
  – *Proverbs 16:3*

- Out of His glorious, unlimited resources, He will give you the mighty inner strengthening of His Holy Spirit.
  – Ephesians 3:16
- Call me and I will answer you, and will tell you great and hidden things which you have not known.
  – Jeremiah 33:3

- Let us, therefore, draw near with confidence to the throne of Grace, that we may receive mercy and may find Grace to help us in times of need.

  – *Hebrew 4:16*

- And all things, whatsoever ye ask in prayer, believing, ye shall receive.

  – *Matthew 21.21*

The Road Less Travelled

When things happen without any rational or logic, one begins to wonder that there is a powerful force originating outside of the human consciousness which nurtures the spiritual growth of human beings?

Yet, we cannot locate this force. Apparently, this force seems to exist beyond the boundaries of the single individual. Mostly, origin of Grace is ascribed to God, believing it to be literally God's love. Grace emanates down to man from an external God. On the other hand, Grace emanates out from the God within the centre of man's being.

Irrespective of how we ascribe the origin of Grace, millions of 'miracles' which take place every day from time immemorial are indicative of its definite existence. Human life and its ongoing process of evolution is its most credible proof. Perhaps, God is the ultimate goal of evolution. God is thus actively nurturing us so that we might grow up to be like Him.

Grace is available to everyone but most of us choose not to heed the call of Grace and in fact, ignore or reject its assistance.

Christ's assertion - 'Many are called, but few are chosen' can be better interpreted as - All of us are called by Grace, but only few of us actually listen to the call.